I Choose Love

The A-Z Guidebook for the Spiritual Warrior

The Pathway of the Spiritual Warrior

I Choose Love

The A-Z Guidebook for the Spiritual Warrior

First Published 2019 A-Z of Emotional Health Ltd.

Published by the A-Z of Emotional Health Ltd.

Welcome

I CHOOSE LOVE

The Pathway of the Spiritual Warrior

Dedication

A Personal Thank You

"I wish to offer a personal thank you to the extraordinary people who I have had the privilege to work with over many years.

You have found the courage to walk through my door and to invite me to walk alongside you for a part of your journey.

You have shared your vulnerabilities and your struggles, your fears and your disappointments. You have shared your learning curves, your growths, your successes and allowed me to be witness to the emergence, evolution and fruition of new hopes and dreams.

You have shown me time and again, that when we truly desire change, regardless of where we have come from and regardless of what may have taken place in our lives, when we step up and embrace our own life from a position of self-responsibility with a commitment to live through kindness, compassion, care and above all, respect, the landscape of our world, both inner and outer will change."

Contents

Introduction

Emotions and the Language of the Heart.

Where do you 'feel' love?
... in your Mind? ... or in your Heart?

So much has been written about the power of the mind. But a human life is not an intellectual concept!

Our core inner identity and what it means to be a 'self', the very substance of who we each are as unique individual human beings, is not simply defined through a process of logical thought. Our core inner values and the things that matter to us are a direct result of the way that we feel. They are a direct result of our emotional experience.

Our greatest lessons in life come not only through our good experiences but also through those events that challenge us and push us to our limits.

Our emotions inform us, they let us know what is going on in our world, whether easy or challenging! If we are closed to our emotions, perceiving them either as something bad, to be squashed and denied, or as an enemy within, something to do battle with and to control, then as far as I can see we are in trouble. To process our life experiences and integrate them into our bank of inner knowledge and wisdom, our extraordinary mind will need to identify and understand our emotions and respond appropriately.

By appropriately, I mean respond in a way that will enable us to navigate our experiences, so that regardless of the actual circumstances, after the event, we will always come away feeling good about ourselves.

In essence, regardless of the actual circumstances, our core self-esteem, not only remains intact, but flourishes and thrives, even in the face of adversity.

Self-esteem plays a key role in our ability to navigate our lives successfully. Healthy self-esteem creates an internal foundation of inner solidity which enables us to develop our durability, our resilience and our confidence. Whether we are wading through the tough times, or we are preparing to launch ourselves into the territory of the unknown in order to discover and step into our fullest potential, we need a platform of solid ground to stand on. This is self-esteem.

When we understand life as a multitude of dynamic experiences, each one shaping our sense of self and contributing to the autonomous adult that we are becoming, each one an opportunity for our Soul to awaken to a higher level of consciousness, then the building and the establishing of our self-esteem takes on a whole new meaning.

Becoming a “self”, a unique and individual “I”, is not an end goal, it is an ever-evolving process

When we discover a way of living that enables us to build within ourselves the solid ground of self-value and self-esteem, built not of external stuff, but of internal values, built of the stuff that matters... we can step into our fullest potential as individual, autonomous human beings. Each of us a soul, learning to navigate human experience with an appreciation of the learning to be found in every moment.

The contents of these pages are a reflection of my own learning and the result of some hard-earned life lessons. A pathway of living, born of being pushed, stretched, sometimes with ease, and sometimes unwillingly and with resistance, to new and more conscious levels of understanding.

Within these pages I share with you an A-Z code of living that I have come to trust. A series of messages that support and guide, creating an ethos of living that continually align us with our higher knowing and the deeper inner voice of our Soul.

This is the pathway of the Spiritual Warrior.

Autonomy

Our capacity to discover our fullest Adult Emotional Wellness lies in the Acknowledgement and Appreciation of our Autonomy.

Autonomy does not mean separateness from the world, it means relatedness with the world.

We are each a unique individual with the capacity for free will and conscious choice.

Whilst we are separate from others in that we have an ability to think independently, we are simultaneously inseparable from all that is life and therefore all that we are collectively a part of.

The roots of true Authenticity stem from this Awareness.

When we are conscious of this extraordinary paradox and can stand in Awe of both the power that we each hold individually alongside a humble Awareness of our smallness within the bigger picture, we can begin to navigate our daily lives from a position of enhanced self-responsibility.

We become Active participants in the creation of our own life story; fully relational, fully alive, vibrant flourishing human beings, present to ourselves, to others and to the energy of life that flows through us, connecting us to all that is 'One'.

Be Brilliant!

Be great today... Be Brilliant...
But not at the expense of anyone or anything else!

People who really flourish do so because they feel good about themselves.

They live honorably and decently, their thoughts, words and actions are founded in respect and genuine regard. As a result, regardless of events and circumstances in their lives, they come away from any situation feeling good about themselves.

The moment our actions involve maneuvering or manipulating others at their expense it is ultimately we ourselves who pay the price. There is no self-respect in stepping on someone else to achieve one's own ends.

Go about your daily life... Do everything from a position of striving to Be the very Best that you can Be.

Whether you are hanging out the washing, cleaning up, making a sandwich, performing life-saving surgery, listening to someone or simply taking time just to 'Be'.

Cultivate an attitude of Being the Best that you can Be, right now!

Celebrate yourself for Being extraordinary in an ordinary way. Your Brilliance will radiate into the world and create more change than you possibly ever imagine.

Thank you for Being Brilliant!

Choice and Change

See yourself as the source of Change in the world.

Each and every day we are faced with a multitude of Choices and decisions.

The way that we think about life, the things that we say and the things that we do, our thoughts, our words and our actions, all have an impact.

Once something has been said or done we Cannot Change it. We CAN however decide what we wish to do… right now.

It is within the immediacy of any given moment, the immediacy of now, that we hold our greatest Capacity for personal Choice and therefore our greatest Capacity for personal power.

In all areas of your life, right now, cultivate an attitude in which you Consciously Choose to live from a foundation of Compassion and Care with an ownership and an awareness of the potential impact of your personal Choices, on yourself and on everyone and everything that you come into Contact with.

The Choices and the decisions that we make today are actively Creating the shape of our tomorrow, influencing not only the immediacy of our own lives, but way beyond our visible horizons.

It is within the immediacy of our own lives that we each hold our greatest Capacity to Create real and lasting Change in the world at large.

Healthy Disappointment

Learn to appreciate Disappointment. It is a gift and a navigational aid that supports you on your journey.

Disappointment is an emotion that contains within it the seeds of potentiality and personal empowerment.

When we experience Disappointment, it means that something hasn't gone well, or at the very least it hasn't gone as we would have liked it to. In truth this presents us with a profound opportunity for conscious and well-informed choice.

When disappointment hits, it can hit hard! We can so easily drown in the intensity of this emotion. When we are hurt and Disappointed by someone or something we understandably see them as the source of our distress, experiencing ourselves as helpless and at the mercy of something outside of ourselves. This is disempowering.

Alternatively, we can listen to this emotion.

Disappointment is a signpost. It is asking us to put the brakes on! To pause and to reflect before deciding how best to proceed.

When we remove judgment of either ourselves or others and we learn to listen to our Disappointment as an opportunity to ask questions, we can begin to use this valuable emotion as a navigational tool. We can use the information it brings to enhance our capacity for conscious reflective Decision making, opening new windows of opportunity for empowered considered choice.

When understood and embraced, Disappointment is a friend and an ally on your journey.

If you are struggling with disappointment, in

"Mindfulness Meets Emotional Awareness
7 Steps to Learn the Language of your Emotions"

a full Chapter is dedicated to this powerful emotion, with pragmatic exercises specifically designed to help.

Additional resources including free meditations for emotional support and emotional release can be found in Jenny's FREE on-line audio/video library

www.azemotionalhealth.com

Empathy

Develop your understanding of Empathy, not simply as a listening skill that you offer to others, but as a Spiritual Pathway of living, enhancing all aspects of who you are and who you wish to become.

If as adults we are the author of our own experience, then how do we become fully present and fully available to navigate our journey through life with conscious intention?

How do we find ways that will enable us to be actively and consciously co-creative, mindful of our choices and indeed mindful of the consequences of our choices?

The answer is Empathy.

Empathy isn't simply a listening ear and something that we can offer others. In essence, true Empathy is a state of being. When we live Empathically, we can relate with our full experience of life at a level of mindful and conscious awareness. Awareness of ourselves, awareness of others, and awareness of a greater, universal intelligence of which we are an integral and dynamic part.

Empathy is the very fabric of relatedness.

Living through Empathy IS living through relationship. It is about being fully relational, and fully present to our entire experience.

When we engage with life through empathy we create a relational connection with life itself.

Empathy is...

... Pure Empathy is an ability to become a fully relational, fully alive, vibrant flourishing human being, able to listen not only to others, but to ourselves and to the energy of life that flows through us, connecting us to all that is 'One'.

When we live our lives through Empathy, we see life and are living life from a foundation of kindness and compassion which in turn supports us in becoming more than we already are and offers the same to all those that we come into contact with.

Spirituality is...

... Spirituality is a state of living, or a state of 'being' in which, in each and every moment, within our everyday human lives, we develop a deep respect for the journey of our soul within the human experience underpinned by an ever-evolving awareness that we are all 'One'.

Our thoughts, our actions and our words demonstrate our desire to live in a manner that benefits all of humanity and the world at large. We aspire to become more than we already are, and we desire to live in a manner that honors this Oneness.

An extract from "7 Steps to Spiritual Empathy, a practical guide". The Spiritual Philosophy of Emotional Intelligence.

Healthy Fear

The first step in learning to manage both Fear and Anxiety is to understand the difference between Unhealthy Fear and Anxiety and Healthy Fear and Anxiety.

In its primary capacity, fear brings us the gift of protection, and therefore the gift of safety.

This may seem an extreme contradiction to our actual experience of fear, because when we feel fear, we don't feel safe... we don't feel safe at all! But when we feel fear, it is actually informing us of a lack of safety.

Healthy fear is an immediate and fully present experience. It is a response to something that is happening right here and right now. When we experience a genuine and real threat, it is absolutely essential that we listen to our fear and we take action!

If I were out walking and a car careered off the road, my healthy fear would activate immediately and, fueled by adrenaline, I would get out of the way. Without fear, self-preservation would be absent.

When a pride of lions sets out to hunt, the animals they are hunting immediately move into high alert. They experience fear, and this is appropriate.

However, when the hunt is over, and fear is no longer needed, they turn their alert system back down again, and within a very short space of time, they will be grazing as normal, often not far from the pride of lions who just half an hour previously were an immediate and very real danger. The threat is over, and they are continuing with their lives.

They do not constantly look over their shoulders anticipating the next attack, never relaxing and never recovering from the ordeal. Nor are they living in a state of denial, dissociated from fear in a way that renders it inactive, leaving them vulnerable to attack when the lions next set out to hunt.

As human being's we are different. One of the difficulties that we can run into in our relationship with fear is that we often lack the skills to self-regulate its intensity and its duration.

When we experience fear, we don't necessarily turn the volume of our high alert system back down automatically. Once our fear has been activated, even though the threat is over, and the same situation may be highly unlikely to ever happen again, we go over and over it in our mind, unable to shake it off and put it behind us.

How do we change this? How can we define a difference between healthy Fear and Anxiety and unhealthy Fear and Anxiety?

A good starting point is to differentiate between the kind of fear that is felt in the immediacy of a moment, when a threat is very real and very present such as being involved in an accident, or being under any form of genuine threat, as opposed to the kinds of fears that we hold within us and within our mind, such as fear of the unknown, fear of failure, fear of catastrophe and disaster, fear of abandonment, of loss and death... the list is endless.

The difference sits in 'the fear of what might be' as opposed to 'the fear of what is'.

The text above is an extract from "Mindfulness Meets Emotional Awareness, 7 Steps to Learn the Language of your Emotions".

If you are struggling with any form of Fear or Anxiety, the full Chapter of this book contains detailed in-depth information about these emotions with pragmatic exercises specifically designed to help.

Additional support including free meditations for emotional support and emotional release can be found in Jenny's FREE on-line library

www.azemotionalhealth.com

"If we find ourselves challenged by strong and overwhelming emotions, our feelings can be so intense that we can feel as though we ourselves are out of our own control.

This in itself then tends to generate further anxiety and fear about the way that we're feeling.

If we 'feel bad' - about 'feeling bad' then inadvertently we generate a secondary package of emotion on top of an already challenging experience.

If we become 'anxious or angry... about feeling anxious or angry' then we have just doubled the emotional load!

This is such a common experience and is incredibly unhelpful for us. The last thing we need at times of emotional difficulty is to make ourselves feel even worse!

The key to changing this lies in our ability to learn to press a pause button: to notice and to listen without adding further anxiety or fear to the mix and to re-evaluate our situation from a position of considered choice."

Gratitude

Embrace the transformational power of Gratitude.

I have read that scientists can measure the energetic frequency of a thought, and indeed the energetic frequency of an emotion.

Gratitude is both a state of mind and an emotional state of feeling.

When we dwell in Gratitude as a foundation for living we create a powerful connection between both Mind and Emotion. A working alliance within us that is centered in a shared vision... and this is a vision of powerful transformation.

Gratitude honors and values the growth and the learning to be found in every precious moment of our lives.

Whenever we look at an experience through the lens of gratitude, we are by default seeking to discover that which we can appreciate and value. Regardless of the actual circumstances the arrival of gratitude will transform our perception of a situation and therefore the way that we feel about it, thus changing the energetic frequency of both thought and emotion.

Even when we are faced with challenge and adversity, when we can discover within ourselves the learning and the growth that has come from this, then in spite of the circumstances, we transform our experience of difficulty into one of personal gain loaded with appreciation and value.

And not only do we develop an appreciation of the learning curve inherent in every situation, but in giving our full attention to the union of both thought and feeling in any given moment, we are actively developing a healthy collaboration between our mind and our emotions.

This collaboration enhances our capacity to become mindfully conscious of the choices available to us in any given situation reinforcing our position of personal power.

Making a conscious choice to live through Gratitude enables us to embrace our fullest capacity for personal empowerment and positive transformation.

Honesty

Live your Life on a foundation of Honesty.

Be Honest in all of your dealings, and above all… be Honest with yourself.

We all mess up sometimes, we're human. However, whilst we cannot change the past or undo any of our past actions, we can always choose what we wish to do about something right now.

If we deny what we ourselves have done and we justify it, either to ourselves or to others, at the end of the day, deep down inside of ourselves, we will always know! Presenting a version of events to the world that isn't true will erode our self-respect and our self-esteem.

Honesty embodies respect, of ourselves, as well as others and is an aspect of Love.

If we have genuinely made a mistake or our actions have resulted in a problem, then this is a personal call to action. Look at the situation through the eyes of both Love and respect and ask yourself, what can I do about this?

When we can put our hand on our heart and know that in any situation we have done everything within our power to address the situation, knowing that we have handled things with absolute Honesty and decency, then even if others portray you in a bad light, presenting a version of events deliberately designed to put you down, then regardless of this, you have every right to feel good about yourself.

Whenever we have made amends and an apology is not well received, then the inability to forgive and to move on is not our problem to carry.

Celebrate your Honor.

Celebrate your Integrity.

Your actions create a beacon of light in the world.

Integrity

Set an Intention to live your life in Integrity.

Be your own hero. Make an agreement with yourself to live a life of Integrity in which you become your own source of Inspiration.

Who do you admire?

Who do you respect?

Who do you find Inspirational?

Who are your heroes?

In my world, the people that I find Inspirational, those I look up to and aspire to be like and who evoke the deepest of respect from within me, are all people of Integrity.

Their achievements may or may not be known in a public way.

Some of them have achieved extraordinary things and serve as a public Inspiration to many of us. Others however, live an ordinary life in an extraordinary way, generating change and creating profound difference in the immediacy of their own world. They are unsung heroes, unknown, and yet without question are held in equal reverence in my heart.

The one thing they all have in common, is that at some point in their lives, they have faced some sort of challenge. They have struggled, overcome difficulties, and most importantly, their actions in response to their difficulties have shone with Integrity.

Integrity is the birthplace of possibility, the birthplace of our fullest potential to develop the hero within ourselves.

Being able to stand firm and remain true to our core values in the face of someone or something that is not okay, whilst owning our vulnerability with honesty and humility is a strength beyond measure.

This is integrity!

Always know that your mind and your thoughts belong to you and you alone. If someone shows us how to behave badly, we can be better than that!

The silver lining of adversity is that it frequently becomes the origin of the changes that we aspire to bring into the world and therefore the very source of the light that we are able to bring to others.

Judgement or Joy

What will you choose to bring into your life?
Judgement or Joy?

We are not defined by the actions and the judgements of others; we are defined by what we choose to do in the face of them.

If you find yourself judged by someone, please remember, their judgement does not define who you are! It simply defines them as someone who needs to judge!

When people make a judgement or speak negatively about someone else it is far more likely to be a reflection of themselves than of the recipient of their judgement.

In my experience, the judgement of others is frequently rooted in envy. A person who judges others has yet to step up into their full potential and rather than rising to this challenge and finding inspiration in those that have succeeded in life, they resort to putting them down.

For a short while in my own life, I lived amongst a group of people whose ethos and culture was to actively do as little as possible to forward their own lives, whilst bemoaning the fact that others had more than they did. Anyone who achieved was demeaned and verbally degraded, usually behind their back, even if that person had worked excessively hard, going above and beyond the extra mile to create their success.

In the course of my entire life, this is the only group of people that I have ever walked away from in their entirety. Their collective ethos was so powerful that even those within that circle who knew that this behavior was not okay were afraid to speak out for fear of being targeted themselves.

Our capacity to literally En-Joy the achievements of others and recognize any underlying feelings of envy as a source of inspiration and an opportunity to broaden our horizons is without doubt a mark of maturity within our own evolutionary growth and worthy of celebration in its own right!

Consider using both Judgement and Joy as a barometer of discernment in all of your relationships.

How much Joy can someone share with you? How much can they celebrate your achievements... indeed how much can they celebrate their own?

On a scale of Zero to One hundred, with Judgement and negativity sitting at the Zero end of the scale and Joy and celebration at the other, consider where each of the people in your life might sit on this scale.

If someone sits either on or close to zero and demonstrates no inclination to evolve beyond this point...

Thank them for helping you develop your skills in discernment...

Send them love...   ....and walk away.

Kindness

Be Kind to everyone and everything... including yourself.

Kindness, like gratitude, is one of the extraordinary emotional states that contains the potentiality and opportunity for bringing about deep and profound transformation.

Kindness is an emotional state of being that alters the energetic frequency of our relational exchanges. When kindness is thrown into the mix a negative situation transforms into one of immense positivity.

If gratitude offers us the opportunity for an internal experience of transformation in which our perception of a negative becomes something that helps us to consolidate our core values, then Kindness offers us the opportunity to live and to demonstrate these values in real terms within our real everyday actions. Kindness therefore brings us a gift of profound personal growth and development.

When we approach a situation through the lens of Kindness then inherent in this transaction we find compassion and a desire for understanding.

Kindness centers us in an internal process of non-judgmental enquiry.

In a potentially re-active situation in which challenging emotions run high, then Kindness will help us to press a pause button fueling a desire to look more deeply, shaping our interactions with others in ways that benefit all parties including ourselves.

Despite its soft and gentle nature Kindness is also firm and strong. Being Kind does not mean that we condone behavior that isn't okay!

Saying No in an unhealthy situation is the Kindest thing that we can do. It validates, acknowledges and identifies a problem, therefore creating an opportunity to initiate a change.

And this could be in response to someone else… or to ourselves!

Our kindness demonstrates an appreciation that there will be some reason beneath the problem, whilst simultaneously demonstrating our absolute support and dedication to work this through.

When kindness becomes the foundation through which we navigate our relationships, what might previously have been a judgement becomes a caring evaluation. What might previously have been a criticism becomes a helpful and supportive critique.

If every single person on this planet lived their life through Kindness the face of this world would change.

We have this choice.

Look for the Learning

There is no such thing as a wrong decision!

Everything that is taking place in our lives in every moment, every happening, every event and every person that we meet, brings us an opportunity to Learn and to grow.

When a tree holds firm in the face of a storm, unseen and below the surface, it is the depth of the roots and the strength of the core that grows from them, that keep it grounded.

Our core values may not be visible to the world at large, however, when in every moment we Look for the Learning we can appreciate that the sum total of our life experiences have created the growth and consolidation of our core inner values, helping us to develop the strength to stand firm in any situation.

When we have an appreciation of what we have gained, even from adversity, we will discover meaning from experience.

When both gratitude and kindness become our personal mission statement in Living a Life that celebrates our capacity to Learn, our past becomes the very the core of our inner strength, the roots of who we have become, integrated within us in ways that strengthens our resilience and our durability.

When we Live with an appreciation of the Learning that is being gifted to us in every moment. When we truly know, not simply as a concept within our mind, but deep in our hearts, that there is no such thing as a wrong decision, only the learning and growth to be found in our development from this position, we embrace our full evolutionary potential to become all that we can be.

Isn't that just amazing!!

Mistakes

Learn to cherish, value, and appreciate Mistakes.
Your own as well as those of others.

None of us learned to walk without ever falling over, our first words were not spoken eloquently and fluently.

How many parents remember the very first words that their children attempted to speak, and the delight we experience in hearing them, and our passion in supporting their learning curve as they gradually formulated words with clarity, building them into meaningful sentences.

And yet we rarely offer this same attitude of appreciation, love, support and sheer enjoyment to ourselves and indeed others on the greater learning curve of our adult lives!

Why?

It is as though once we become adults, we are supposed to have it sorted! We are supposed to know exactly what to do, what to say and how to get it right. Judgement and criticism kick in and become the inner voice that accompanies and oversees our daily actions and engagement in life.

Gently and kindly manage yourself with an enjoyment and an appreciation of your strivings and a delight in your Mistakes. Your Mistakes are the birthplace of your personal growth and development!

Wisdom and Maturity are not marked by our years. They are marked by our ability to learn from our Mistakes and to integrate this learning into our future actions.

Non-Judgmental Enquiry

Develop within your mind, an internal environment of Non-judgmental Enquiry.

Judgement and criticism damage confidence and lower self-esteem.

The naming, blaming, shaming game, whether of others or of ourselves, does not foster any form of healthy accountability. In fact, it does the opposite! It creates an environment in which people are afraid to make mistakes, fearful of being targeted, humiliated and punished.

If through fear and judgement we learn to hide our mistakes, this actually denies us the opportunity to learn from an experience.

However, removing any form of criticism whatsoever also denies us the opportunity to grow from our mistakes.

We remove the opportunity for healthy evaluation, to be 'real' with ourselves, to do better, to strive to be more, and to truly enjoy the fulfilment and the self-respect that comes from knowing that we genuinely did our best, especially when we then succeed.

Change your inner critic to an inner critique.

Cultivate an attitude in which mistakes, your own and those of others, are appreciated and valued for the learning curve that they bring.

With a healthy critique, a Mistake becomes a gift that supports us in becoming even more than we already are.

Ordinariness

Develop your ability to notice and to treasure the Extraordinariness of Ordinariness that is within you and all around you.

We all know that it is the little things in life that matter.

And yet as adults we frequently get caught up in evaluating the nature of personal success through the bigger targets and external goals that we believe we should be achieving. We rush around, wishing we had more time, and yet never stop to see that which is immediately available to us.

Cherish every moment of your day and every moment of your life. You are precious, and your life is a gift.

And do not concern yourself with getting old, there are many who are not afforded this opportunity!

At least once in every day bring your attention to the present moment and allow yourself to stand in awe and in wonderment at the multitude of things that you are gifted with.

A smile... a thank you... an unexpected act of kindness... the smell of the rain... birds flying in synchronicity... the stars...

Notice how these everyday occurrences leave you feeling and make a commitment to create more of the same yourself. It is my experience that the greatest changes, that make the greatest difference in the world at large, take place within the 'Ordinariness' of our everyday, real lives.

Honor your own capacity to manifest Extraordinariness in all of your actions. In doing so you embrace your own unique ability to Be the cutting edge of change in creating the kind of world that you wish to see.

Be Ordinary in an Extraordinary way!

Problems

Consider viewing any kind of Problem as an opportunity rather than a Potential crisis.

Every Problem contains within it the source of a Potential resolution.

Whenever we identify a Problem, our very recognition and acknowledgement of this difficulty creates an opportunity to seek a potential solution.

To work out what we can do about it, how we might address this situation, where we might go to seek answers and what avenues may be available to us to Potentially arrive at a resolution.

As long as a Problem remains unseen, unrecognized or indeed denied, then the doorway to any Possible solution remains closed.

When faced with a Problem or difficulty or a challenge within our adult lives, what we each choose to do in response to this challenge can make the difference between a Problem being compounded and repeated or alternatively worked through, resolved and used as a valuable learning curve, creating significant and lasting change.

In this we have a choice.

When we shift our Perspective and our attitude towards Problems, not only do we ourselves grow from the situation but we also demonstrate to all those around us that a Problem is not something to be feared, rather something to embrace and value for its cherished Potentiality.

Quietly Ask Questions

Learn to be Still... Learn to Listen... and stay in the Questions.

Whenever you experience uncertainty or overwhelm, it is time to find some Quiet within yourself.

It is time to be still... and it is time to listen!

Take a particular situation and give yourself time and space to listen.

Listen with your ears.

> What information are you hearing? Factual information, words, language, tone of voice? Listen?

Listen with your eyes.

> What are you seeing, what can you 'hear' with your eyes? What actions are taken? Are they the consequences and the result or outcome of previous actions? Is there a repetition of a pattern or similar behavior? What emotions are visually present? What body language do you see? Can you see a re-action rather than a re-sponse? Listen?

Listen with your body.

What is your "gut feeling" telling you? Where in your body are you experiencing this situation? We experience emotions in our physical body, in fact there are many sayings that give us clues about the way our body carries emotional experience. We "shoulder" responsibility. It got "under my skin". I had a "lump in my throat". What emotions are present and where do they sit within you? What are they saying to you? What is their story? Listen?

Listen through your heart.

What do you feel in your heart? What are the emotions and feelings that are channeling through your heart? What is your heart telling you? Listen?

Listen with your mind.

What do your thoughts tell you? We all have an inner dialogue. Is your mind critical of the situation? Critical of either yourself or others, or are your thoughts positive, encouraging and supportive? Do your thoughts anticipate the best or the worst outcome? What are your thoughts telling you to believe? What kinds of beliefs and values are your thoughts generating and reinforcing? Listen?

This is part of an exercise from "7 Steps to Spiritual Empathy, a practical guide", designed to enhance and develop your ability to Learn to Listen.

Listening gives us good information and this information is there to give us assistance and to inform active and conscious decision making, choices that spring from a foundation of conscious self-awareness. Awareness of ourselves, awareness of others, and indeed awareness of the bigger picture, awareness of our environment and world around us.

Give yourself permission to be curious and learn to stay in the Questions.

Know and appreciate that what you think you know in this present moment can always be extended by a Question. We can always discover more.

An attitude of discovery without judgement or blame will create an environment of success regardless of the outcome.

Respect and Appreciate your Mistakes.

TREASURE AND VALUE YOUR MISTAKES

THEY ARE THE CUTTING EDGE OF YOUR PERSONAL GROWTH...
THE FRONT LINE OF YOUR EVOLUTION

Respect

Even though we cannot see it, Respect is something that we can feel. It is a tangible and yet unseen experience.

Hopefully most of us will know what it feels like to be treated with Respect, even when faced with a difference of opinion, however, I suspect, with sadness, that most of us will also know what it feels like to be on the receiving end of a lack of Respect or an inability on the part of another to consider our thoughts and opinions as valid, regardless of agreement.

Like many qualities, Respect can be open to misrepresentation and manipulation. I have come across instances where Respect is a word that is used in a way that I would consider to be inappropriate.

Someone once told me that they respected their father, when in fact as our conversation emerged it became apparent that they feared their father.

Respect born of fear is not true Respect.

True Respect denotes care and regard. True Respect symbolizes the health and well-being of our own sense of entitlement, as well as our recognition and desire to support and validate the entitlement of others.

True Respect acknowledges and validates the differences between us and therefore our unique individuality, indeed true Respect celebrates difference.

It gives definition within relationships where both similarity and disagreement can be validated; a space where agreements can be discussed, negotiated and made, even if those agreements are in celebration of a difference of opinion.

True Respect, acknowledges and validates our right and our opportunity, to discover and formulate our own opinions, to develop our ability to reflect and to make our own conscious choices; and it acknowledges and validates the rights of others to do the same.

Respect enables difference to be welcomed with interest, rather than received as a threat and as something to be defended against, and this creates possibility for learning and for growth. Doorways are open, and there is a mutual flow of both giving and receiving.

Living Respectfully means living honorably.

Even when faced with inappropriate action on the part of others, in living Respectfully, we demonstrate by example.

Our intentions and our actions are the birthplace of manifestation. If we wish to live in a world that holds Respect dear, then we will need to live Respectfully.

We have a choice.

An extract from "7 Steps to Spiritual Empathy, a practical guide".

Self-Care, Self-Love & Self-Responsibility

Self-care is a gift to Humanity. When we embrace Self-care, we embrace Self-responsibility. And when we look after ourselves, we have an abundance to give to others.

Self-care has always been a challenge for me!

Given that I am an experienced Counsellor with over 26 years of experience, this may not make a lot of sense, surely, I should know about this stuff, this is my area of expertise? But I can tell you firsthand that there is a big difference between helping other people to learn to take care of themselves and helping ourselves to take care of ourselves!

Enabling other people on their developing journey of Self-care came easily to me, however applying the same principles to myself did not.

Looking after myself and prioritizing my own well-being felt selfish and not only did I feel selfish, but the idea of putting myself before others seemed completely contradictory to my core spiritual belief in being a kind and giving person.

This was then compounded by everything that I had read about the law of attraction.

Surely being a giving person should bring giving people into my life!

And yet here I was … giving and giving and giving even more, to the point of heading for burn out! And yet what I needed wasn't coming my way. In fact, if anything, I was finding the complete opposite!

My solution… When giving went wrong I would try to give more!

It was a light bulb moment for me when I realized that by not looking out for myself, I was not showing myself any form of respect and was therefore attracting into my life people who also didn't show me any form of respect.

Until I demonstrated care for myself, I would not attract anyone else who would demonstrate care for me.

Until I listened responsively to my own needs, I would not attract others into my life who would wish to listen and be responsive to my own needs.

And so began my own journey in understanding the true nature of healthy Self-care! A pathway of living that would enable me to listen and be responsive to myself.

7 Steps to Spiritual Empathy, the first book in my series about the Intelligence of our Emotions, is the result of this learning.

A series of steps actualizing the core principles that empowered me to live a life of genuine Self-respect and Self-care without compromising my core Spiritual beliefs.

Self-care is not an Act of Selfishness…

It is an Act of Consciousness!

Trust

There is a direct relationship between Self-esteem, Emotional Resilience and Trust.

Emotional resilience in adulthood doesn't come from having a perfect and happy existence with no ups and downs in life.

Our emotional durability and resilience in the face of human life challenges, stems from a core of healthy self-esteem built upon a foundation of Trust.

As children we are dependent upon the adults around us to respectfully acknowledge and validate us in ways that support and teach us to navigate our lives with a reasonable degree of confidence and durability.

This includes the validation and management of the full range of our emotions. We need to be able to successfully navigate the stepping stones of natural developmental growth without experiencing emotional overload and overwhelm.

This experience of knowing that we will be okay even if we don't feel okay right now, creates an internal sense of stability, with an underlying innate sense of Trust which in turn becomes a foundation for the development of healthy self-esteem.

Whilst validation from others is extremely important, as self-aware, empowered adults we have the opportunity and the choice to be in charge of this for ourselves.

Each and every day, validate ANY and ALL of your achievements, however big and however small!

We all know that many small problems left unattended will create a mountain of difficulty, generating anxiety and undermining our belief that all will be well.

The same principle applies in reverse.

Many small steps, validated and celebrated daily, will create a mountain of achievement, constantly reinforcing an inner sense of Trust that will build and maintain durability, self-worth and self-esteem.

Understanding

A great many of the problems faced by humanity would change if every situation was approached with a desire for Understanding.

Understanding enables us to travel beyond the constraints of assumption and perception.

In our desire to find Understanding we are seeking to find meaning and we open ourselves to this possibility.

Developing meaning in life is not just a mental process... it is not simply a question of thought. A genuine evaluation of any situation will involve not only the way that we and others think about something, but also the way that we both feel. We must be available to listen to both mind and emotion.

When we listen to life through our logical thinking, we are engaging with the intelligence of our mind. When we listen to life through our emotions, we are engaging with the intelligence of our heart.

We need both, not one at the expense of the other.

The presence of our emotional voice in collaboration with reflective, considered thought, creates opportunity not only to hear and appreciate the position and viewpoint of someone else, but also to reach an understanding of our own position and present this with a willingness that overcomes differences and bridges any gaps of misunderstanding.

Understanding is a dynamic and expansive state of being.

Fueled by respect, Understanding expands our consciousness, taking our external vision and awareness into new territory, whilst simultaneously deepening our inner vision and insight.

When Understanding becomes our guiding light… our north star… the intelligence of our mind can dance with the intelligence of our heart, expanding our knowledge and awareness, escorting us to new levels of consciousness.

Values

Live in accordance with your own true inner Values.

Be yourself. Walk to the beat of your own drum. And when you find your own song, sing it with pride.

Whatever our unique and individual pathways, try to be true to your own, whilst actively demonstrating your respect for the unique and individual pathways of all others that you come into contact with.

Sometimes our nearest and dearest, our families and our friends, believe wholeheartedly that they know what is best for us. Their intentions are honorable. They desire only the best for us. However, their perception of what is best is often limited to the realms of their own personal experience.

The choices and the decisions that they desire for us will be a reflection of their own unique and individual journey, a picture of the conclusions that they have come to on the basis of their own life experiences.

There is no malice within this, the dreams that they hold for us stem from a foundation of love.

In truth if we are to journey through this life from a position of ongoing developing autonomy, we will each need to discover our own unique and individual pathway.

Stand tall and allow your own journey to unfold as it should.

As long as your pathway demonstrates an absolute respect for others, you will discover your own song.

The Power of Words

Be mindful of your Words, they carry power!

As a writer and someone who has come from a talking profession, I have come to understand the power of Words. They are the tools of my trade.

Why are Words so powerful?

It is never simply the intellectual meaning, or the concept portrayed, but the feeling and the emotion contained and carried within them. Words carry the power, the energy and the influence of emotions.

A powerful and charismatic speaker can ignite an audience, enflaming and awakening a passion that can fuel and incite action. Actions of destruction… or actions of peace!

Words can hurt: "You're stupid!" "You're pathetic!" You'll never amount to anything!"

Or they can heal: "I'm so sorry… that will never happen again!"

Words can bring joy: "Wow, that is just amazing!" "I adore you… " "I love you… "

And what of empty Words?

Empty Words are not empty of either power or emotion, as a general rule, they are empty of action!

When we talk about empty words, we are describing a situation where actions are not congruent with what has been said.

The Words will still carry power and emotion, but the emotional content will have changed.

"I'm sorry" might evoke happiness, gratitude and appreciation, perhaps even relief.

However, "I'm sorry" followed by the same thing happening again, will evoke completely different emotions. Disappointment, sadness, frustration, maybe even fear.

Consciously choose to take charge of your Words, not only in what you say to others but also in the way in which you speak to yourself.

They carry power and they have an impact.

X-Ray Vision

Develop your ability to look beyond the obvious and the immediate.

The scope of our human vision is limited, not only by the constraints of our physical eyesight but also by the perceptions and viewpoints that we hold in our minds eye. Make an agreement with yourself to strive to always look beyond the obvious with a desire to understand and to look more deeply. This is reflection.

Take some time each day to reflect.

True reflection asks us to free ourselves from any loaded preconception or assumptions and to take time to really hear and consider all aspects of an experience.

True reflection involves objectivity, a state of being where we enhance our ability to be both present and yet an observer at the same time, to feel deeply involved and yet un-involved in the same moment, to care and yet simultaneously hold an objective viewpoint.

When we occupy a space of reflection we sit in paradox because as a space of learning and possibility it is by its very nature a place of movement and potential growth, and yet it is also a place of stillness, peacefulness and quiet.

Reflection is never a busy place.

Embracing true reflection is a one of the most valuable tools that we have available to us. It enables us to notice. Whenever we notice something, we create a window of opportunity in which our deepening awareness can inform our conscious thinking and direct our actions.

The Art of Saying both Yes & No

Learn to say both Yes and No with discernment.

Do you ever find yourself saying Yes when really you should have said No?

And then when you do say No you end up feeling guilty about this?

Sometimes the greatest gift that we can offer someone is to say No.

If I were a teacher with a class of 30 children and there was a bully amongst them, it would be of absolute importance that I step in and say No! But my No wouldn't only be to ensure an environment of protection and safety to the class. I would also be offering protection to the bully as well.

My No would be accompanied with a desire to look more deeply and discover the origins of their behavior.

We do no-one any favors if we allow their bad or inappropriate behavior to continue.

By not acknowledging the problem we become complicit in supporting their actions, denying them the opportunity to overcome whatever difficulties have caused them to be this way in the first place.

When our No is delivered with the strength of firm and loving kindness, we create an experience of safety that validates a true value for all concerned. We are demonstrating how to set clear and strong boundaries, boundaries founded in love, respect and regard.

No is a boundary. A boundary that denotes care, compassion and respect.

Sometimes the greatest gift that we can offer ourselves is to say No.

When we say a big healthy No to ourselves, if we are engaged in any form of self-destructive behavior, we are showing ourselves respect and we are engaging in genuine self-care. We are actively involved in developing our own healthy limits and our own healthy boundaries.

Yes and No walk hand in hand and are essential ingredients in our capacity to maintain the healthy boundaries that define us as empowered autonomous individual human beings.

Saying No to any form of abuse or any form of destructive or damaging behavior whether in others or within ourselves is a statement of health.

When we say No to something or to someone unhealthy, we are saying Yes to life!

Zen, Zeal, Zest, Zing, Zenith

Be Brilliant! Be Extraordinary!
Make a commitment to yourself, to live your life "In Love".

Pause for a moment… and be still.

Cherish and treasure this moment. All that surrounds you. All that you are. All that is.

Quiet your mind. Quiet your emotions. Find within yourself a point of Zen. A place of stillness and deep connection and presence yourself within this experience.

Be still…
…and listen.

Consider that alchemy is NOT some chemical transformation that changes lead into gold, but rather the extraordinary Golden Opportunity granted to us each for the transformation of our Soul within the journey of our human life.

And what is it that makes a human life such a perfect vessel for the evolution of the soul?

It is the very imperfections of our humanness that make us so absolutely perfect!

Our mistakes, our failures, our struggles, our challenges, our steepest learning curves, each a window of opportunity to be embraced with Zeal and Zest and Zing…
…or indeed resisted.

And in this we have a choice.

Cast your mind back. Be an observer of the life that you have lived. Not only the joys, the laughter, the love, but also the heartbreaks and the shadows that we would prefer to forget. All are treasures of immeasurable value in their contribution to the extraordinary person that you are today.

Love your mistakes. They are the cutting edge of your evolution. As are the mistakes that others have done to you.

Honor your intention to live in integrity and become your own source of Inspiration. Navigate your life through the eyes of love. And always look for the learning.

Be Brilliant! Be Extraordinary!

Be the gift that you are, and you will discover your Zenith, your own North Star, your inner guiding light in the quest for the transformation and the evolution of your soul.

Zen. *A form of Buddhism emphasizing value of meditation and intuition.*

Zeal. *Persistent endeavor. Earnestness in furthering and advancing a cause or rendering service.*

Zest. *Keen enjoyment or interest, relish gusto.*

Zing. *Vigor energy.*

Zenith. *A point of heaven is directly above the Observer. A point in either time or place of greatest power, prosperity and happiness.*

A Message of Gratitude

"It is my experience that the greatest changes, that make the greatest difference, take place within the 'ordinariness' of our everyday, real lives.

When faced with a problem, a difficulty or a challenge, what we each choose to do in response, our attitudes toward the situation and our subsequent actions, can make the difference between a problem being compounded and repeated, or alternatively, worked through, resolved and laid to rest.

In this we have a choice.

Thank you to all of you, who in the extraordinary ordinary ways, that are so often unrecognized and yet make such a difference, choose to live as you do. In doing so, you create a beacon of hope for others to follow."

Namaste

"If Our Eyes are the Windows of Our Soul, then Our Emotions are the Voice of Our Soul."

Jenny Florence.
Born 1961, Counsellor, Writer, Speaker

About the Author

Jenny Florence worked as an Accredited BACP, UKRC Registered Counsellor for over 26 years. She has written several books including 7 Steps to Spiritual Empathy, Mindfulness meets Emotional Awareness, 7 Steps to Learn the Language of your Emotions and the I Choose Love Series which includes the Art of Manifestation Oracle Cards. She first began reading Runes and Tarot cards as a teenager and has also studied Astrology.

She is the founder and creator of the A-Z of Emotional Health on-line Video Library, a free Public Resource, understanding Emotional and Mental Wellness from a holistic perspective.

https://www.azemotionalhealth.com/

You can also follow her on Social Media

Youtube – https://www.youtube.com/c/AZEmotionalHealth/

Facebook - https://www.facebook.com/azofemotionalhealth/

The Pathway of the Spiritual Warrior

Made in United States
North Haven, CT
09 November 2022

26496240R20046